Well-being
Coloring Book

Aryla Publishing 2021

978-1-912675-99-9

www.arylapublishing.com

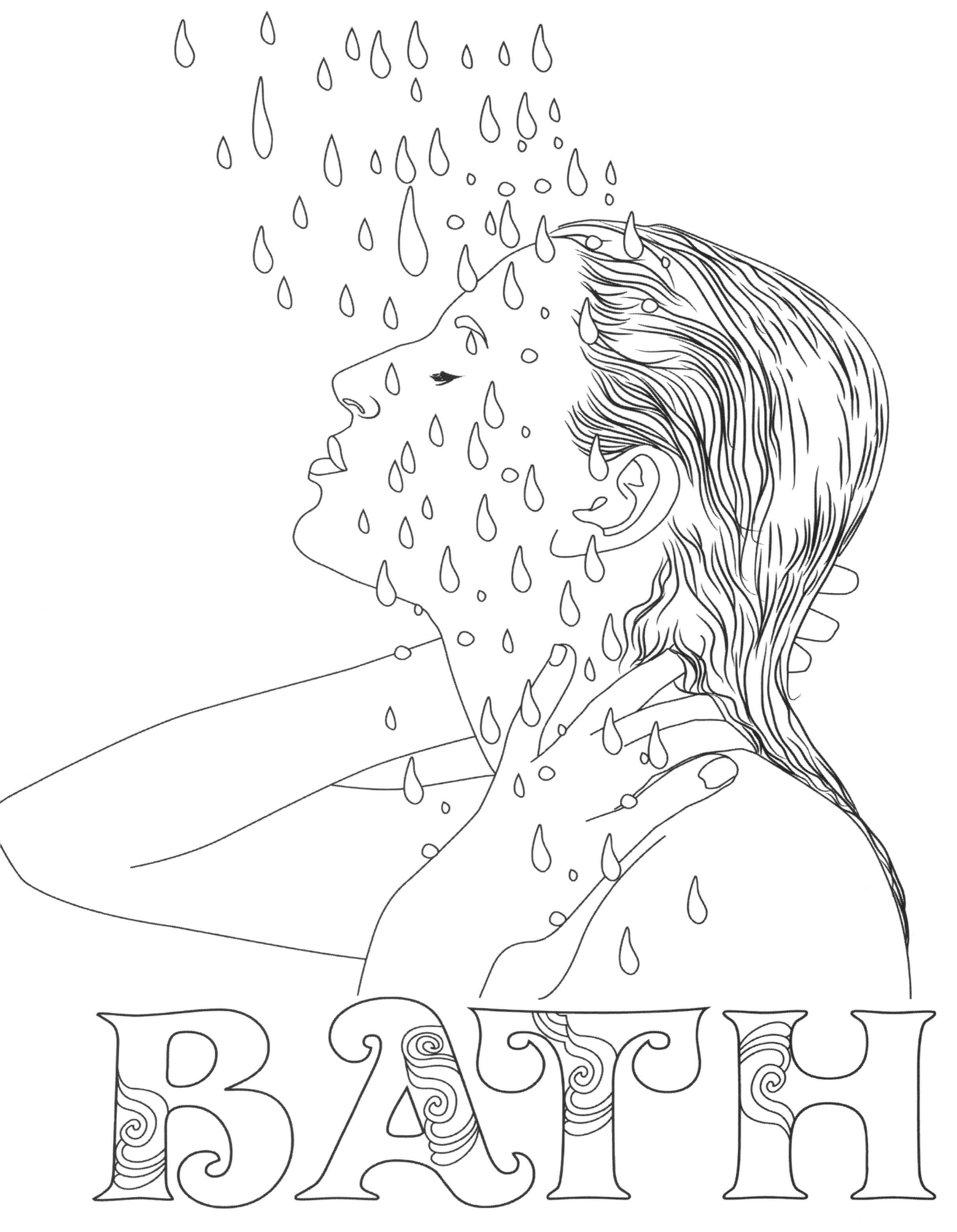

Exercise

Thank you for purchasing this book.

If you would like to know more about Aryla Publishing Books please visit:-

www.ArylaPublishing.com

Or follow us on
Facebook
Twitter
Instagram
for *free promotions*

@arylapublishing

We would love to know what you think of this book so please leave us a review.

Have a wonderful day ☺

Other Coloring Books from Aryla Publishing

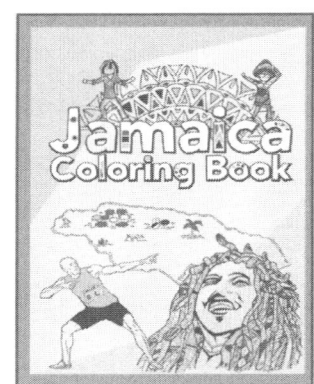

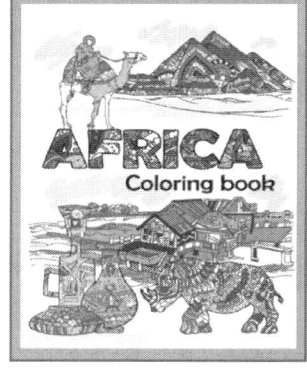

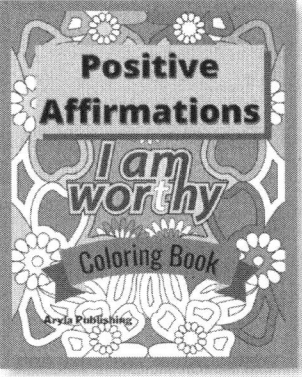

Color In Fun
Kids Books

Visit **www.ArylaPublishing.com**
to find out about all new releases.

Follow us @arylapublishing on Twitter Instagram & Facebook

Search for Aryla Publishing on

 YouTube

Check out our _Book Trailers_

Subscribe **to keep up to date with new releases!**

WE WOULD LOVE YOUR FEEDBACK

PLEASE LEAVE REVIEW AT:-

Printed in Great Britain
by Amazon